Along the River Cray:

a pictorial history of the Cray Valley

by

Katherine Harding and Denise Baldwin

No part of this publication may be produced, stored in a retrieval system,
or transmitted in any form by any means, electronic, mechanical, photocopying, recording,
or otherwise without prior permission of the Head of Libraries and Community Information

© 2003 Directorate of Corporate Services

ISBN 0 902541 70 6

Cover: Waterside, Crayford, c1910

This book is dedicated to the people who have lived and worked along the Cray and who have made it the historical gem it is today.

A poor life this if, full of care,
We have no time to stand and stare.
W.H.Davies (c1911)

Contents

	Page
Introduction	7
The Source at Orpington	9
St Mary Cray	21
St Paul's Cray	33
Foots Cray	41
North Cray	61
Map of Kent showing rivers Cray and Darent, 1719	68-69
Bexley	81
Crayford	97
Barnes Cray	117
Crayford Marshes	125

Introduction

This book looks at a river: short in length, approximately 9 miles, but one, nevertheless, that is incredibly diverse. It is a river of great character which has given rise, during its long history, to towns and villages, lovely churches and a variety of industries including milling, brick-making, tanning and dyeing and a range of crafts such as basket-making and boat-building. These, together with a mix of colourful personalities who have lived near the river, make it a fascinating area to explore, not just for its past but for what it has to offer us today, for it is still a vibrant feature of our local communities.

There are references to the Cray as early as 785 when Offa, the King of Mercia, gave some land named Craeges Aewlma to one of his vassels, a man called Ufa. According to Hasted, Craeges Aewlma means river spring and the river takes its name from the Saxon 'crecia' meaning a brook or rivulet. However, more recent research suggests that Cray comes from the Celtic word 'crei' meaning fresh or clean. In the centuries that lay ahead, the Cray was to be recognised for its good supply of clear, sparkling water, a supply abundant enough and sufficiently fast-flowing to allow the building of several mills that brought work to the inhabitants of the villages along its way, no less than five of which actually take their names from the river itself.

The Domesday records of 1087 show that eleven mills existed between Orpington and Crayford and, over the centuries, high quality paper, silk, book-binding cloth, textiles, cereals and flour have been produced in these mills. The presence of the River Cray as a source of power has indeed shaped the industries of our communities beyond Domesday.

The Source at Orpington

The Source at Orpington

The first sight of the Cray is at Orpington Ponds in the Priory Gardens. There is a variety of wildfowl attracted to this area and the ponds have only dried up once, in 1898, since records began. Around the ponds are weeping willows, flowering cherries and some exotic shrubs including a New Zealand cabbage tree and eucalyptus.

The Priory is a misnomer as it was never a monastic establishment. Much of the building has gone but the Great Hall still remains and is now a museum, adjacent to Orpington Library. In the Domesday Book it was referred to as land of the monks of the Archbishop of Canterbury and its three watermills with villagers and smallholders provided a good living: so much so that William the Conqueror's half brother Odo seized the land around the Priory but had to return it a few years later to the church after a three-day trial. Odo owned much land along the Cray and has been described in history as rapacious and cruel.

Records date back to a house here from 1270 when Hugh de Mortimer, the first rector of Orpington, lived there. It was a high-status building constructed partly in stone and timber-framed and was used by important officials of the Archbishop of Canterbury. Edward II stayed at the Priory and is the only recorded king to have done so. In 1573 Elizabeth I came to visit Sir Percival Hart who had built a house on a hill overlooking the Cray, although his main residence was Lullingstone Castle. He was Chief Server and Knight Harbinger to Henry VIII, an office he retained through to the reign of Elizabeth. In order to please his sovereign, it is said that he arranged a pageant on the river which included a mock sea-battle involving small ships called barques. It was Elizabeth I who named Sir Percival's home, Barque Hart; eventually Bark Hart. The church of All Saints, endowed in 1173, now much changed, was alongside the house.

In the 17th Century Orpington Priory was owned by the Hon. Richard Spencer who added an extension. He was an ardent royalist who loaned Charles I £60,000 but he was captured and, at his trial, his lands were confiscated and he was exiled from Kent. Sadly, with the return of the monarchy in 1660 and despite petitions, the Priory was not restored.

In the 1930s the Priory was owned by the Hughes family and Mrs Hughes was keen to establish her garden using some of the ideas of her friend Gertrude Jekyll.

An outdoor theatre was created where amateur plays were performed to local people. This still survives in the grounds which are open to the public.

In 1947 Orpington Urban District Council bought the building and in the 1960s much of the 19th Century building, considered to be of no architectural merit, was pulled down although it is now thought that some of the older building was lost in the demolition.

The Cray turns north-east to disappear under a culvert by the A224 opposite Carlton Parade. Originally, a mill known as Colegate Mill, later renamed Hodsolls Mill, stood here and watercress grew in abundance. Following the construction of the Orpington by-pass in 1923, this area attracted a great deal of light industry due to the good water supply, its proximity to London, good building land and a suitable workforce. Even today it is a mecca for large outlets dealing in carpets, electrical goods, household appliances and furniture. A riverside walk takes this gently flowing river into St Mary Cray.

A pictorial history of the Cray Valley

1. The river's journey begins at Priory Gardens, 1989.

2. Orpington Priory, 2002.

Along the River Cray

3. Monk's Walk, Priory Gardens, Orpington - but no monks walked this way! Undated.

4. A view of The Priory taken from the garden. Undated.

5. *The Hall at Orpington Priory. A mismatch of styles gives a comfortable feel to the entrance hall. Undated.*

6. *The Priory and Public Library, 1961.*

7. "Bark Hart", Orpington. Legend has it that Sir Percival's dogs kept Elizabeth awake when she stayed here. Could that be the origin of the name? Undated.

8. All Saints Church, Orpington. Little remains of the original church. Undated.

A pictorial history of the Cray Valley

9. High Street, Orpington, looking south-west. Undated.

10. High Street, Orpington. Coronation procession for George V, June 1911.

11. High Street, Orpington c1900. Truly a bygone age when a lady could safely cross the road! This photograph is taken looking north from the village hall.

12. Hodsolls Mill, Orpington c. late 1890s.

13. The waterwheel underneath Hodsolls Mill, 1934.

St Mary Cray

St Mary Cray

The village took its name from the church of St Mary the Virgin, once surrounded by a prosperous farming community. The present building dates from around 1250 and was restored between 1861 and 1895. It is believed that the church is built on the site of a Roman encampment and Roman tiles and pottery have been found in the lower portion of the bell tower. The church has many treasures, a notable one being the 15th Century Italian oak screen separating the chancel and the Hodsoll chapel, named after a local farming family. The church is also known for its seven brasses, the earliest of which is the Avery brass of 1568.

Until the reign of Edward I the village was known as South Cray. In 1281, Edward gave rights for a weekly market to be held here and a substantial area was given over for this purpose. A small patch of green known as Market Meadow is all that remains today but, until the early 18th Century, St Mary Cray had a market house on this plot of land.

Hasted described St Mary Cray as a "handsome and populous village" with the river being always central to the life and industry of the inhabitants alongside the Cray. The river's course has been altered by developments over the centuries, often being hidden in narrow culverts. In the 19th Century, it was renowned for the purity of its water due to the proximity of its underground source and it was once famed for its trout. The village has long been recognised in more recent times as an industrial area with a population, until the late 19th Century, larger than Orpington. However, the whole area was surrounded by orchards; apple, cherry, pear and plum and there were also hopping and strawberry fields with most of the produce from all these enterprises going to Borough Market. The produce was usually taken by horse and cart late at night; a journey taking several hours but, later, it was transported by road.

Milling was the oldest established industry in St Mary Cray. In the 18th Century, one mill produced paper. Milling became a thriving industry as the village's close proximity to London guaranteed raw material and a market for the finished product. In 1833 William Joynson took over the mill and turned to the production of high quality security paper used for bank notes and stamps, amongst other uses. As the century progressed, rail became used for transport and so increased opportunities to obtain new raw materials. In the 1930s it made hygienic food-wrapping and other industrial papers and was later taken over by the Wiggins Teape group when it produced vegetable parchment. With the growing use of plastics in the food industry in the 1970s, the mill became obsolete and was eventually demolished.

The railway viaduct of nine arches was built in 1858 to link the Chatham and Dover routes and was one of the probable Nazi targets during the bombing raids of 1941. It remains a distinctive landmark today.

The lake in St Mary Cray, known locally as the Blue Lagoon, was part of a planned garden estate and open-air swimming pool, opened in 1933, which attracted many day-trippers from London who came down by train at weekends. Jack Doyle, the boxer, trained here during some of the winters in the 1930s. Badly damaged in the war, it is now used for private fishing.

14. Two landmarks of St Mary Cray – the railway viaduct and the church of St Mary The Virgin. Joynson's Mill would have been to the right of the photograph, 1995.

15. St Mary The Virgin. It is believed that the church is built on the site of a Roman encampment and Roman tiles are embedded in the lower portion of the bell tower, 1988.

16. Joynson's delivery van. Joynson's was an important employer for the local inhabitants of St Mary Cray. Undated.

17. Joynson's Paper Mill. The only recognisable landmark now is the 1858 railway viaduct. Undated.

A pictorial history of the Cray Valley

18. St Mary Cray looking south, c1900. The viaduct of nine arches was built to link the Chatham and Dover routes. It was probably a target for the German bombing raids of 1941.

19. Dancing Bear in Angelsea Road c1900. One cannot help but feel sorry for this unfortunate creature.

20. High Street, looking south. The police station entrance is on the left. Note the buildings on the right with their typical Kentish weather boarded fronts. Early 1900s.

21. Post Office, 82 High Street, St Mary Cray. Undated.

A pictorial history of the Cray Valley

22. High Street, St Mary Cray looking south, c1960.

23. High Street, St Mary Cray opposite the church, 1962. The building is jettied giving a good clue to its age.

24. Demolition of Viaduct Cottages. The old Engine House dated 1830 is in the foreground, c1950.

25. St Mary the Virgin, the Parish Church of St Mary Cray. This would once have been at the heart of village life with the river running alongside it. Undated.

26. The Avery Brass in St Mary Cray Church. The largest figure is about 30cm high. The inscription reads: Of your charity pray for the souls of Richard Avery, Joan, Agnes and Elynor his wives which deceased 11 day of July the year of Our Lord 1568. On whose souls thou have mercy.

27. The waterfall in the Riverside Gardens, part of the mill run. Undated.

Along the River Cray

28. Many happy an hour spent by London day-trippers at the "Blue Lagoon" Swimming Pool in Cray Avenue, 1933.

29. Much of the river is now culverted through St Mary Cray. The chimney on the right belonged to a former smithy and is now demolished. Undated.

St Paul's Cray

St Paul's Cray

The Cray travels through to the adjoining parish of St Paul's Cray described by Hasted in the late 1700s as having no village, just fifty houses dispersed along the river. There were three water-wheels here, one for dressing leather in oil and two for grinding corn. The modern village sign shows the church, a mill, the Kent white horse and an apple, the latter reminding us that there were once orchards in surrounding fields.

St Paulinus Church derives its name from the Christian missionary, St Paulinus, the first Archbishop of York, who came to Kent in 601. Built in flintstone, the main structure dates back to around the early 1200s although an earlier church is mentioned in the Domesday Book. Roman tiles are clearly visible in the stonework and, during the last war, while building an air-raid shelter, a Roman brick kiln was discovered. The church is now deconsecrated and is a Grade I listed building.

In 1824, Thomas Nash, whose father had been a paper-maker in Hertfordshire, leased a paper-mill and started a dynasty, which was to last for almost 150 years. It was a difficult time for paper-making as there was an excise duty on paper but, after many improvements, which included installing machinery in 1828, the mill began to prosper. After his death at the age of 44, the mill continued to be managed by his sons and it became the chief employer of the area. In 1914, the mill was making rag papers of a durable quality for bank notes. During the First World War it carried on as usual, but was faced with the problem of shortage of labour as many of the mill workers had migrated to the munitions works where wages were higher. One of the Nash sons, Gordon, became a flight instructor but was killed on a training flight over Kent in 1918. The mill suffered bomb damage during World War II and, after a takeover, it finally closed in the 1960s.

Along the River Cray

30. The River Cray looking towards Nash's paper mill. July 1965.

31. High Street, St Paul's Cray, c1900 showing The Bull Public House and the Post Office on the right.

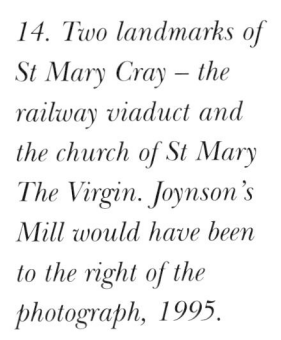

14. Two landmarks of St Mary Cray – the railway viaduct and the church of St Mary The Virgin. Joynson's Mill would have been to the right of the photograph, 1995.

15. St Mary The Virgin. It is believed that the church is built on the site of a Roman encampment and Roman tiles are embedded in the lower portion of the bell tower, 1988.

Along the River Cray

16. Joynson's delivery van. Joynson's was an important employer for the local inhabitants of St Mary Cray. Undated.

17. Joynson's Paper Mill. The only recognisable landmark now is the 1858 railway viaduct. Undated.

A pictorial history of the Cray Valley

18. St Mary Cray looking south, c1900. The viaduct of nine arches was built to link the Chatham and Dover routes. It was probably a target for the German bombing raids of 1941.

19. Dancing Bear in Angelsea Road c1900. One cannot help but feel sorry for this unfortunate creature.

20. High Street, looking south. The police station entrance is on the left. Note the buildings on the right with their typical Kentish weather boarded fronts. Early 1900s.

21. Post Office, 82 High Street, St Mary Cray. Undated.

22. High Street, St Mary Cray looking south, c1960.

23. High Street, St Mary Cray opposite the church, 1962. The building is jettied giving a good clue to its age.

24. Demolition of Viaduct Cottages. The old Engine House dated 1830 is in the foreground, c1950.

25. St Mary the Virgin, the Parish Church of St Mary Cray. This would once have been at the heart of village life with the river running alongside it. Undated.

26. The Avery Brass in St Mary Cray Church. The largest figure is about 30cm high. The inscription reads: Of your charity pray for the souls of Richard Avery, Joan, Agnes and Elynor his wives which deceased 11 day of July the year of Our Lord 1568. On whose souls thou have mercy.

27. The waterfall in the Riverside Gardens, part of the mill run. Undated.

Along the River Cray

28. Many happy an hour spent by London day-trippers at the "Blue Lagoon" Swimming Pool in Cray Avenue, 1933.

29. Much of the river is now culverted through St Mary Cray. The chimney on the right belonged to a former smithy and is now demolished. Undated.

St Paul's Cray

St Paul's Cray

The Cray travels through to the adjoining parish of St Paul's Cray described by Hasted in the late 1700s as having no village, just fifty houses dispersed along the river. There were three water-wheels here, one for dressing leather in oil and two for grinding corn. The modern village sign shows the church, a mill, the Kent white horse and an apple, the latter reminding us that there were once orchards in surrounding fields.

St Paulinus Church derives its name from the Christian missionary, St Paulinus, the first Archbishop of York, who came to Kent in 601. Built in flintstone, the main structure dates back to around the early 1200s although an earlier church is mentioned in the Domesday Book. Roman tiles are clearly visible in the stonework and, during the last war, while building an air-raid shelter, a Roman brick kiln was discovered. The church is now deconsecrated and is a Grade I listed building.

In 1824, Thomas Nash, whose father had been a paper-maker in Hertfordshire, leased a paper-mill and started a dynasty, which was to last for almost 150 years. It was a difficult time for paper-making as there was an excise duty on paper but, after many improvements, which included installing machinery in 1828, the mill began to prosper. After his death at the age of 44, the mill continued to be managed by his sons and it became the chief employer of the area. In 1914, the mill was making rag papers of a durable quality for bank notes. During the First World War it carried on as usual, but was faced with the problem of shortage of labour as many of the mill workers had migrated to the munitions works where wages were higher. One of the Nash sons, Gordon, became a flight instructor but was killed on a training flight over Kent in 1918. The mill suffered bomb damage during World War II and, after a takeover, it finally closed in the 1960s.

30. The River Cray looking towards Nash's paper mill. July 1965.

31. High Street, St Paul's Cray, c1900 showing The Bull Public House and the Post Office on the right.

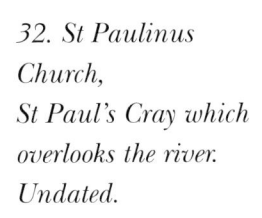

A pictorial history of the Cray Valley

32. St Paulinus Church, St Paul's Cray which overlooks the river. Undated.

33. River view of St Paul's Cray. In Norman times St Paul's Cray was a manor given to Odo and worth £4 a year. Undated.

34. "The Bull Inn", St Paul's Cray. A familiar watering hole! Undated.

35. William Nash Limited (Paper Mill) at St Paul's Cray, 1965. Thomas Nash, the founder of the paper mill, died in 1845 and is buried in St Paulinus Churchyard.

36. The village sign shows the church, a mill, the Kent white horse and an apple reminding us that many orchards once surrounded the village, 2000.

Foots Cray

Foots Cray

The river, having left St Paul's Cray, moves on to the village of Foots Cray and it can be clearly seen at the Seven Stars, a former coaching-inn whose records date back to 1717. An early inn sign showed a Madonna's head surrounded by seven stars and an old plaster cast of this, found during excavations, now hangs inside the pub. The river was once fordable at this point and previous owners of the inn would have regularly been called on to light the way through the water for late-night travellers on the main road from London to Maidstone. The present bridge is Georgian, but has been modernised.

Once a picturesque rural Kentish village, a mill had been recorded on this site as far back as the 11th Century. The last one, founded by Benjamin Harenc, stood from 1767 to 1929 and for some 20 to 30 years had been a silk mill. In the late 19th Century the mill turned to white paper and envelope-making. It had two water-wheels and had obviously been considered worth mechanising; thus steam was introduced to supplement the water power by 1840. Later it was involved with textiles again with the printing and dyeing of flags and the manufacture of book-binding cloth. It was a weather-boarded, timber-framed, 3-storey building on the present Fujitsu site. The 1851 census shows that it employed 30 men, 30 boys, 30 girls and 80 women, many of whom were Irish immigrants who had come here during the famine of the 1840s. Living conditions were not good; about 29 people in one dwelling, and the average age of inhabitants was 20. From 1895 to 1905, the mill was used as a laundry. By 1910, the steam plant had been demolished and electricity was used to provide power. A major use thereafter was making cameras, films and artificial silk, until Mr E.K.Cole took it over for the manufacture of wireless sets before moving to Essex, where he founded the EKCO radio firm.

Foots Cray Place was undoubtedly the grand house of the area in the 18th and 19th Centuries. A lovely Palladian building, it graced the area now known as Foots Cray Meadows for almost two hundred years before sadly being destroyed by fire in 1949. Fortunately, many of the beautiful trees planted in the gardens and grounds of the house still remain to delight today. Prior to that, an Elizabethan manor house, Pike Place, is indicated on a map of 1683 situated by the river behind All Saints Church. The house had belonged to the Walsingham family for six generations and was still standing in 1772.

All Saints Church, with its lovely views, is a beautiful spot to stop at. With its 14th Century stone and flint walls, it occupies the site of a former Saxon church and would have replaced an earlier building of wood and thatch. Entering the churchyard by its Victorian lych-gate, we are reminded of the Saxon practice of resting the corpse in the gate before proceeding into the church for the burial service (lych is a Saxon term for corpse). Other than two 14th Century windows, there is little evidence of earlier times but in 1862 and 1863, during renovations, two lead coffins were found under the floor and another in the south aisle. The remains of twenty people were discovered in the Sanctuary and, under a brass plate dated 1400, a bunch of lavender was also discovered with its stalks intact. The spire was given by Lord Waring to commemorate the coronation of Edward VII in 1901 and there are five bells in the tower, which are regularly rung. The baptismal font of Purbeck marble is Norman and pre-dates the church.

All Saints boasts a notable and beautiful churchyard which, over the last few years, has been carefully and lovingly tended, with stones being repaired and cleaned. In 1896, the churchyard was extended with land from the Foots Cray estate as the village population had risen substantially since the early 1800s. The most interesting gravestones are to be found in the older part of the churchyard, particularly the iron grave slab to Martin Manning dated 1656. The headstone to Elizabeth Bennett, who died in 1781 aged 22, carries a poignant epitaph and no hint of Mr Darcy!

Unpierced by any dart but death
I quick resigned my fleeting breath
My roses withered ere t'was noon
Alas why blown to fade so soon
Then virgins learn from hence your fate
How frail is all your blooming state

The Harenc family were owners of Foots Cray Place and local benefactors, and some members of the family are commemorated on a vault in the churchyard. The largest and most impressive monument, however, is a stone Celtic cross to Sir John Pender and his family. Sir John was a pioneer of the transatlantic submarine cable and had lived at Foots Cray Place for a number of years.

The lovely Georgian five-arched bridge, recently restored and renovated and with an ornamental lake behind, is a well-known landscape feature in Bexley. The river flows through this very attractive and picturesque landscape, which has established walkways and large open areas for the public to enjoy. There is a variety of birdlife with the renowned parakeets alongside herons, kingfishers, swans and moorhens. The Meadows also enjoys a diverse flora.

37. Seven Stars Public House, a 'traditional village pub' according to 'Cobbetts Rural Rides', c1910.

38. Ambling home. Foots Cray Lane now Rectory Lane, c1920.

39. Foots Cray Place. One of the grander houses along the river. During the Second World War it was used by the training ship HMS Worcester, 1947.

40. All Saints Church, Foots Cray. Built on a Saxon site, the earliest parts date from 1330. The spire was given by Lord Waring to commemorate the Coronation of Edward VII. The churchyard is beautifully kept, c1912.

Along the River Cray

41. Foots Cray before the invasion of cars, very much a working village with the countryside within easy reach, c1900.

42. The lake at Five Arches, an idyllic setting, 1960.

A pictorial history of the Cray Valley

43. Five Arches Bridge, recently renovated, is one of the jewels of Bexley Borough, c1960.

44. Foots Cray National School. The new school building was built in 1882. At one time children had to pay 1d. a week and were sent home if they did not bring it. One local man remembered his school days at the beginning of the 1900s as "just a bit of chanting"! Undated.

45. Foots Cray Mill which was demolished in 1929. The mill had many uses, from silk printing to envelope making. A Sun Life policy of 1798 listed the mill as having a kiln, water wheels, rag culling engines, a pump, a rag house and a dwelling.

46. Footpath beside the River Cray in Foots Cray Meadows, c1965.

47. The Pender memorial in All Saints churchyard, 1990. Sir John Pender was a pioneer of the transatlantic submarine cable and had lived at Foots Cray Place for a number of years.

48. This print shows a picturesque church in a lovely setting. In early times the church was on the border of Chislehurst as there were no churches in Sidcup then. Undated.

49. Catt's Corner, Foots Cray c1912. The Barley Mow was one of seven public houses in Foots Cray.

*50. The Seven Stars was another! It has records dating back to 1717.
Was the hatted gentleman in the front a 'song and dance man'? This photograph is dated 1910.*

51. This was the main road from London to Maidstone and the Seven Stars, on the right-hand side of the photograph, was an important staging inn before the coming of the railways. This is one of our favourite photographs, c1910.

52. The entrance to Rectory Lane is on the left and Cray Road is on the right. Can you spot the Red Lion Public House? c1950.

53. High Street, Foots Cray, looking up the street from just beyond the bridge, 1928. Bridge House is on the left opposite the Seven Stars Public House on the right.

54. The banked area on the left was the garden of the Seven Stars Public House. The mill had been demolished by this time, c1930.

55. STC Business Systems, 1983.

56. Foots Cray Mill Workers, c1918. At that time the mill was producing silk.

57. Looking down Rectory Lane, formerly known as Foots Cray Lane, towards All Saints Church in the distance, c1920s.

58. Reshingling of Spire of All Saints Church, Foots Cray c1939. There are five bells in the tower and because of the 1860s alterations they are usually rung from the centre of the nave.

A pictorial history of the Cray Valley

59. All Saints Church, Foots Cray in the winter of 1962. Notice the change of road name.

60. Foots Cray Place, 1928. This view shows the west side. The remnants of the fountain can still be seen today.

61. There were extensive gardens at Foots Cray Place. This photograph taken in 1928 shows the Dutch Garden.

62. Foots Cray Place on fire, October 1949. The cause of the fire which destroyed Foots Cray Place was unknown but workmen were working in the building at the time and it is thought a spark ignited from burning paintwork. The dome quickly caught alight.

A pictorial history of the Cray Valley

63. The River Cray running through Foots Cray Meadows, 1960.

64. Children fishing in Foots Cray Meadows c1980s, a pastime no longer allowed much to the relief of the pike and tench!

North Cray

North Cray

On the south side of the river opposite the Foots Cray Place estate is North Cray village which once stretched along both sides of a narrow country road. It was described by Hasted as "pleasant and healthy being situated on a gravelly soil and in a well frequented neighbourhood….the garden of this part of England". Although not especially populous, the village was surrounded by grand houses and prosperous farms. Now it is sadly decimated by the dual carriageway of North Cray Road.

St James', in North Cray, is a striking church which was built in 1852, although there was certainly a church here in the 12th Century and probably before. The church has many treasures including box pews, a carved Flemish reredos from the 15th Century and a delightful modern stained glass window showing the river and Five Arches. There is also an interesting marble memorial to Octavia, Lady Ellenborough who was the sister to Lord Castlereagh.

The church was once the private chapel of the owners of North Cray Place, a large mansion once owned by the Vansittart family but now demolished to make way for housing. In 1812 Nicholas Vansittart became Chancellor of the Exchequer. Although he was replaced by Frederick John Robinson, Viscount Goderich, in 1823, Vansittart was given the title of Baron of Bexley and was made Chancellor of the Duchy of Lancaster in compensation for losing the Chancellorship. Vansittart bought Foots Cray Place in 1822 and North Cray Place in 1833, although he chose to live at Foots Cray. When he died, his funeral at St. James' was the best attended on record.

The area around the Cray abounded with grand houses. North Cray had cheap land with clear water and was close to London thus ensuring it attracted wealthy merchants, bankers and politicians: most notable was Robert Stewart, Viscount Castlereagh and later Marquess of Londonderry. He leased North Cray Cottage with its grounds stretching down to the Cray, as his country house, in 1811. Renaming it Woollets Hall he spent £14,000 on it and, in the outbuildings, he kept kangaroos, emus, antelopes and a tiger. The Cray then had trout and, with a herd of Merino sheep, it created an idyllic setting.

This, however, was not to last. In 1822 Viscount Castlereagh, overworked as Foreign Secretary and leader of the House of Commons, was suffering from paranoia.

He was sent to North Cray to rest but, despite being closely watched, he cut his throat in his dressing room with a two inch penknife. He negotiated the Union with Ireland but his deal to grant emancipation, in return for Catholic support, was repudiated by George III. This change of policy made him many enemies. One such was Lord Byron who wrote "So he has cut his throat at last! He? Who? The man who cut his country's long ago". Castlereagh had wanted to be buried at St James' Church but he was buried in Westminster Abbey between Pitt and Fox. His lovely home has of late been used by the Malcolm Sargeant Trust for terminally ill children, but has now closed. It is to be reopened as a home for adults with learning difficulties.

The picturesque setting around North Cray begins to change as the river flows through small farms to Bexley.

65. North Cray Place Club. Yet another house sadly no longer with us. Demolished in 1962, it had been built in the late 19th century.

66. North Cray Road. Undated.

Along the River Cray

67. Jubilee Cottages, North Cray Road. What price progress? When the North Cray dual carriageway was constructed, the village of North Cray paid the price and only vestiges remain. All these buildings were demolished, including the 18th century almshouses and the former infant school building, c1910.

68. The church of St James' was founded in Saxon times although this building is largely 19th century, c1904.

69. Loring Hall as it was in the 1800s. It was built in 1760 by a gentleman called Neighbour Frith and was then called North Cray Cottage. Some cottage!

70. Vale Mascal. A lovely house that has the added attraction of the river running through the grounds. It also boasts a Victorian bath house. Vale Mascal is now a popular place for civil marriages. Undated.

Along the River Cray

Section of Map of Kent showing rivers Cray and Darent 1719.

A pictorial history of the Cray Valley

Engraved by Samuel Parker for John Harris' History of Kent

71. Perhaps the saddest loss of the widening of the North Cray Road was this weather-boarded, timber-framed 15th century hall house. The significance of this vernacular building was such that it has been reconstructed at the Weald and Downland Open Air Museum near Chichester. This photograph was taken in 1928.

72. A winter scene at North Cray, 1990.

A pictorial history of the Cray Valley

73. North Cray Road in 1979. Some of the original village buildings remain on the left including the White Cross Public House.

74. An earlier view of the North Cray Road, c1920.

75. The Village Stores, North Cray Road, 1967. Jevons' shop was part of the Medieval Hall House.

76. The Rectory at North Cray now sadly gone. Undated.

77. North Cray Place, pre 1915. A rural view indeed! Later the house became ivy-clad and was demolished in 1962.

78. Part of the North Cray Estate. Some of these grand trees still remain, c1980.

79. Loring Hall, 1944. This house, much renovated, overlooks the Cray.

80. Mount Mascal Lodge, North Cray Road, c1900. The lodge still stands today and has been sympathetically extended.

81. Mount Mascal, c1922. A large Jacobean mansion demolished in 1957. It was believed to have been built in the early 1600s. Owned by John Mascal in the Tudor period it eventually passed to the Vesey-Holt family whose graves are marked by monuments in North Cray churchyard.

82. Vale Mascal, North Cray Road. The house, built c1740 on the Mount Mascal estate by Thomas Tash, son of Sir John Tash, an Alderman and ex-Mayor of London, still looks much the same today. It is now licensed for weddings. Undated.

83. Vale Mascal Bath House, c1930. This stands, today, in one of the gardens along the North Cray Road and has been restored.

84. River Cray in Vale Mascal grounds, 1951. In the mid to late Victorian period Rev John Egerton and Rev Philip Egerton took great interest in landscaping the gardens.

A pictorial history of the Cray Valley

85. North Cray Bridge, c1910. The river in some of its more attractive settings as it leaves Foots Cray Meadows and flows towards Bexley.

86. The river at North Cray, c1970. "All along the backwater, through the rushes tall…"

87. The river at North Cray in the winter, c late 1940s.

88. The drive to St James' Church, North Cray. Undated.

89. St James' Church, North Cray, c1928. Described by Hasted at the end of the 18th century as a "small mean building" but during the 19th century it was considerably enlarged into the graceful building we see today.

Bexley

Bexley

The Domesday Book records three mills in Bexley. In medieval times, the mill in the High Street was on the Archbishop's land and one of the heaviest recurring expenses was its upkeep, which was anything between £2 and £7 a year. Meticulous records were kept detailing the purchase of new stones for one or other of the three mills, their transport by water from London to Dartford, the hiring of help to get the stones from the boat to the Archbishop's cart, and the siting of the mill. The cost of the stones was the biggest item and amounted to £2 or £3 or more.

The last mill was built in 1776 and described by Hasted as a corn mill owned by the Lord of the Manor, the University of Oxford; it also ground barley and maize. In Victorian times many changes were made and steam was installed because the water power of the Cray had diminished. In its final years, the mill was used for the storage of sacks. It was destroyed by fire in 1966 and rebuilt as a restaurant.

Bexley church was recorded in the Domesday Book and is dedicated to St Mary the Virgin. Over the centuries many additions and alterations have been carried out and restoration work in 1883 uncovered medieval floor tiles. Replicas of these are now in the chancel floor. The wooden belfry is probably medieval and is known as a 'candle snuffer' spire. In 1775, thieves broke into the church at night and wrenched open the parish chest. Finding no silver communion plate, they cut up the pulpit cloth and stole the communion cloth. Vandalism and wanton damage is not, it would seem, a problem of our present time only. The church houses some fine memorial brasses, one of which, the Hunting Horn brass, is most unusual.

Hall Place is a distinctive part Tudor, part Jacobean country house. Sections of the present house date back to 1540. Sir John Champneys constructed the northern half of the building using stone from monasteries which had been closed by Henry VIII shortly before. Stonework from the 13th-15th Centuries has been found in the walls and many of these are medieval mouldings. Sir John died in 1556 and his son Justinian enlarged the house bringing the stone-built part of the building to its present form.

Mills have been recorded at Hall Place since the time of the Domesday Book. Flag Mill was a large tiled and boarded flour mill behind the stable block.

Around Hall Place, and towards Crayford, the river has developed a large flood plain. In the 17th Century this lent itself to the setting up of the bleaching industry. Merchants were looking for land near to London, unpolluted by smoke, with clear water and enough coppice wood to provide the ash required for the bleaching process. Large areas were cleared, streams diverted, weirs constructed and buildings erected and, within time, this area became well known for its bleaching quality, despite competition from the Dutch. Alongside the river, the textile industry grew, the best known being the David Evans Silk Mills, now sadly closed as the works were relocated to Macclesfield. David Evans was a silk merchant from Shropshire who, in 1843, took over the site from the inventor Augustus Applegath.

Another illustrious textile printer who had connections with the Cray was William Morris who lived at the Red House in Bexleyheath after his marriage in 1859. He stayed there for only 5 years but this time was the happiest period in his life. It was while at the Red House that he set up the Firm which, with its innovative patterns and designs, would revolutionise the Arts and Crafts movement. In 1884, as part of his 'river' chintzes, he produced a sumptuous design called Cray. A most expensive design to produce, a copy hangs in the Red House which has recently been acquired by the National Trust.

90. Hall Place Mill, Bexley. Known as Flag Mill, the building was three stories high and had two water-wheels and four pairs of grinding stones. It was demolished in the 1920s. If you look carefully, you can still see where it stood in the grounds of Hall Place.

91. Bexley Mill, south side, 1949.

92. The Old Mill, Bexley c1933. The mill had an interior undershot wheel which was 10 feet in diameter. This drove four pairs of stones.

93. Restoration of the spire of St Mary's Church, Bexley. Obviously no health and safety rules here! Just look at those precarious positions. In 1853, the re-shingling of the spire cost £85.11s.6d. By 1979, it had risen to £9,000.

94. St Mary's Church, Bexley c1903. In all the churchyards along the Cray, yew trees are a noticeable feature. In pagan times, the yew was dedicated to the goddess of death, ghosts and witchcraft and many of them were grown at pagan sacred sites where churches were eventually built.

95. Hall Place, Bexley, c1990.

96. The river winds gracefully past Hall Place and its gardens, c1975.

97. Feeding the chickens at the rear of Bexley Mill. Pre-1929.

A pictorial history of the Cray Valley

98. Back of the Mill Stream seen from the grounds of Cray House, 1944. Notice the three beehives near the shed.

99. This print, dated 1838, shows St Mary's Church with many interesting external features. The lych-gate situated by the road has now been relocated. From a watercolour by W Dann.

100. St Mary's Church, c1970. Up to the end of the 15th century the floor was earthen and there were no pews. Here the Church is decorated for Harvest Festival.

101. The Hunting Horn brass 1407. It commemorates Henry Castilayn, an important layman and chamberlain in the household of the Bishop of London in 1374. He was a wealthy landowner and, what we would call today, a property developer.

A pictorial history of the Cray Valley

102. Royal Artillery, based at Woolwich, watering their horses at Old Mill, Bexley, c1914-1918.

103. The Manor House, east of St Mary's Church, stands on the site of the Medieval Court Lodge, the administrative centre of the manor. Undated.

104. High Street, Bexley showing Styleman's Almshouses, built in 1755, on the left and the Poor House in the distance. A familiar sight even now, c1910.

105. High Street House, Bexley, c1906. The house was built by John Thorpe, the antiquary, in 1761. He contributed a great deal to the study of the history of West Kent.

106. Hall Place, Bexley, built c1540 by Sir John Champneys, a former Mayor of London. The main building material for the northern part of the house was stone from abbeys which had been demolished following the dissolution of the monasteries by Henry VIII. c1920.

107. Hall Place Mill, 1915.

108. Hall Place Mill, c1906. A mill has been recorded here since 1621 and probably was one of those mentioned in the Domesday Book.

109. Hall Place Bridge, c1910. A delightful scene now lost to road changes and the sound of the A2.

110. On Friday night, 16 October 1987, a hurricane brought devastation to Kent and felled several fine trees at Hall Place.

111. Hall Place Bridge, c1920.

Crayford

Crayford

Crayford is a town steeped in history and much has been written about it. It is recorded in the Anglo Saxon Chronicles that Hengist and his son Esc fought against the Britons at Crecanford and killed 4000 men. Before that, the Romans are thought to have had a military station, Noviomagnus, where the Cray could be forded along Watling Street at what is now Crayford Bridge. In 1396 Richard II visited Ireland with large financial help from the Archbishop of Canterbury. As a reward for this support, Richard, when requested by his loyal primate, granted Crayford a market charter to Archbishop William Courtney. Traces of the old town can still be found in part of Crayford. The bridge was built in 1755 and, at that time, it was turnpiked. The brickwork on the north side of the bridge is dated 1938 and incorporates two stone tablets showing the dates. A tanning factory once stood by this spot. The tannery must have emitted an interesting odour around the town!

Overlooking the Cray, The Bear and Ragged Staff public house occupies a key location. The building dates from 1925 and replaces an older establishment but records suggest there has been a public house of that name since 1704. It takes its name from the coat of arms of the Earl of Warwick who held manors at Dartford and Chislehurst. Cray Gardens, set out in 1938, is a small oasis in the middle of Crayford and it must have been a welcome area in a busy town. A dry drinking fountain is dedicated to S.A.Blackwood who lived at Crayford Manor House and was a prominent evangelist preacher and father of the writer Algernon Blackwood. Behind this area were more industrial units devoted to the calico and silk printing works of Charles Swaisland. Set up in 1824, part of the land was sold to Maxims and then to G.P. & J. Baker who continued with textiles until they closed in the 1960s.

Crayford's industrial history has been of mixed fortunes. In 1881, William Morris visited Crayford with his friend the potter William de Morgan, a specialist in lustreware. They were looking for new premises as their London workshops were too cramped. Old buildings were looked at because they were, according to Morris, "cheap, big, solid buildings," but he was dismayed by the signs of rural desolation in the area and opted to move to Merton.

All this changed somewhat with the arrival of the American, Hiram Maxim, a compulsive inventor and entrepreneur. In 1888, he moved his gun and ammunition factory from Hatton Garden to Watling Street, Crayford to form the Maxim-Nordenfelt Gun and Ammunition Company Ltd. Albert Vickers acquired Maxim's company in 1897 to establish Vickers, Sons & Maxim, where they developed the Vickers Maxim quick-firing machine gun. Sadly, with reduced orders after the Boer War, the factory at Crayford went into decline.

The years 1914-1918 meant that war brought prosperity to Crayford and the workforce at Vickers increased to 14,000. Women were also brought in for lighter machine work such as making shells, fuses and cartridge-cases. Fluctuating fortunes continued until 1939 when Vickers became the biggest single supplier to the navy and was involved in the development of the bouncing bombs of "Dam Buster" fame. By the 1980s, despite much reorganisation, the works closed and a shopping complex was built. The Vickers work's canteen became Crayford Town Hall which, although dilapidated, still remains along with the Clock Tower. This was built by Dartford Rural District Council in 1902 and served two purposes; as a sewage lift station and, bizarrely, to commemorate the Coronation of Edward VII.

Crayford in the early Twentieth Century was still very rural despite its industry. Boating parties passed up from the Thames to visit the tea-gardens, children fished and played with toy boats. It is recorded that the rector from the parish church of St Paulinus, on the hill above the river, would go by boat along the Cray to visit the Joyce Green Fever Hospital at Dartford.

St. Paulinus Church has two naves, one of only three such churches in the country and these naves were built with the vast income from pilgrims who used it on their way to Canterbury and to pray for a safe journey across the heath back to London. Its position on the hill above the town kept it safe from flooding by the Cray.

112. St Paulinus Church was built on a hill overlooking the Cray to avoid regular flooding. The church has two naves which is an unusual feature. c1924.

113. Keeping a careful watch, note the policeman's shelter situated at Crayford Bridge. Undated.

Along the River Cray

114. Cannon and Gaze Flour Mill lorry crashing into Crayford Bridge, 1907.

115. Waterside, Crayford, c1905.

A pictorial history of the Cray Valley

116. Happy days, fishing and paddling in the Cray – at this time Barnes Cray was fields and farmland, c1910.

117. David Evans Silk Mills in Bourne Road. The Cray travels along the top of the photograph. Undated.

118. Aerial view of Crayford showing the river and the old Stadium in 1985. The huge Vickers works can be seen in the top right-hand corner.

119. Crayford Bridge showing the old police box, c1906.

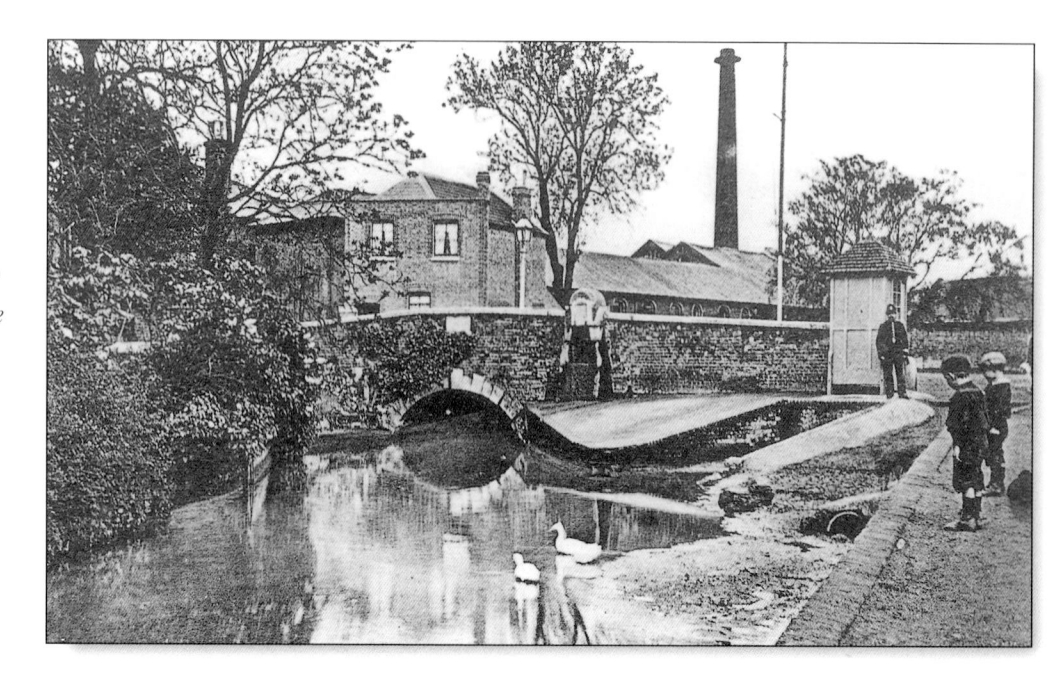

120. Crayford Tannery around the 1900s. The Tannery was situated near Crayford Bridge.

121. Crayford 'Village' looking towards Crayford Way and the beginning of Barnes Cray. Undated.

122. Waterside Gardens, Crayford. Undated.

123. This photograph shows rural dilapidation in parts of Crayford. It deterred William Morris and William De Morgan from choosing premises in the area to develop and expand Morris and Co. products. Undated.

124. Dartford Rural District Council built the Clock Tower in 1902 as a sewage lift station and to commemorate the coronation of Edward VII!

125. Waterside Gardens, Crayford, 1985.

126. Reflections on the Cray, 1951.

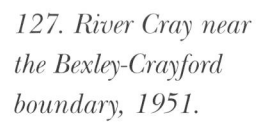

127. River Cray near the Bexley-Crayford boundary, 1951.

128. David Evans Silk Mills, c1975. Hand block printing on silk was a highly skilled, time consuming task, each colour being printed separately! The river's water was used in the rinsing of the silk.

129. David Evans. Silk screen printing by hand carriage allowed a quicker output, c1975.

Along the River Cray

130. Crayford Tannery awaiting demolition in the 1950s. This Tannery was situated on Crayford Bridge opposite the Bear and Ragged Staff Public House. The Tannery was owned by Murgatroyd Brothers from 1911 and was demolished in 1952.

131. The Bear and Ragged Staff Public House, High Street, Crayford, c1930. In the 1990s the pub was renamed The Orange Kipper but after public outcry reverted to its original name.

132. Crayford Bridge showing the Bear and Ragged Staff Public House and Bridge House. The public house building was pulled down and rebuilt in 1925.

133. London Road, Crayford c1916 without a vehicle in sight.

134. The River Cray flowing under Crayford Bridge c1910.

135. St Paulinus Church, Crayford c1905. Parts of the present building date from about 1100.

A pictorial history of the Cray Valley

136. Crayford High Street c1910. The shape of the road looking up the hill is little changed. Most of the houses on the left open out onto the road.

137. Waterside, Crayford, 1905. This was a popular area for Crayford families before Barnes Cray had been developed.

Along the River Cray

138. Manor House, Crayford 1955. This grand white mansion was built in the early 19th century in the Italian style. In the 1870s it was the home of Sir Arthur Blackwood, a local philanthropist.

139. A gentle scene around Crayford. Undated.

A pictorial history of the Cray Valley

140. By the River Cray, Crayford. Undated.

141. Bridge House, Crayford, c1920. The group of hatted gentlemen have time to pose, possibly waiting for the Bear and Ragged Staff to open! Tramlines can be seen in the cobbled street.

142. An aerial view of Crayford, 1929. The river travels through the centre of the picture with the Vickers Works in the foreground. Crayford Way and Green Walk to the north of the river show the houses built by Vickers for their workforce. The Princesses Theatre is in the left corner.

143. Footpath by the Cray, 1951.

Barnes Cray

Barnes Cray

The river leaves Crayford and wends its way through an area known as Barnes Cray, an established hamlet whose name comes from the Barne family, cloth-makers and East India Merchants in the 18th Century and owners of May Place. The Barnes Cray fields were an area of marshland used by the textile industries for bleaching. Many felt that the low lying nature of the area led to sickness known as the ague which afflicted many.

Barnes Cray is said to be the site of Ellam, a medieval manor house that gave its name to a prominent local family, the Ellams. Henry Ellam was Auditor to Henry VI. In 1750 Ellam, May Place and Crayford Manor House were inherited by Miles Barne, whose family gave its name to Barnes Cray.

During the First World War, a 'garden suburb' with over 600 houses, mostly concrete, was built here for the Vickers' munitions workers. A 'folksy' design for these terraced and semi-detached houses was apparent in the prominent gables, central archways, open porches and roofs sweeping down to create dormers. At the bottom of Iron Mill Lane, an iron mill produced plate for armour but the site was subsequently used to build a flour mill which became renowned for its special Vitbe flour which retained the vital vitamin B oils. The Cray was a powerful river in the 1800s and its energy turned a breast-shot water-wheel working five pairs of stones. Nowadays, the old works and pond have disappeared under tarmac and the area is used as a newspaper warehouse.

A so-called iron church, All Saints, Barnes Cray, stood at the conjunction of Maiden lane and Iron Mill Lane between 1917 and 1960. It was a daughter church of St Paulinus, Crayford. When the church closed, a chapel at St Paulinus was named All Saints in its memory.

Sailing-barges with a shallow draft known as 'pitch-piners' were also built in this area. These flat-bottomed craft would have been ideal for navigating the river as the main method of transporting heavy goods was by sailing-barges up the Thames and along the tidal river Darent to Crayford Creek. Various industries grew along the banks of the river at this stage such as 'bricks, barges, nitric acid, flour, sparklets and siphons' as they were described in 1902.

Where the river passes Barnes Cray on the west bank, it forms the boundary between the London Borough of Bexley and the neighbouring Kentish Borough of Dartford.

144. A snapshot of the river at Barnes Cray, 2002. Who would believe this was the middle of suburbia!

145. Time has mellowed these houses built for the Vickers workforce, 2002.

A pictorial history of the Cray Valley

146. The river passing through Barnes Cray, c1910.

147. This photograph is taken from the bridge in Maiden Lane, 1997. The site of Barnes Cray House would be to the right of the river.

Along the River Cray

148. Pen and ink sketch of Barnes Cray House taken from the Opening Ceremony programme of the Princesses Theatre, Crayford on 26 July 1916.

149. Barnes Cray House, 1919.

A pictorial history of the Cray Valley

150. All Saints Church, Barnes Cray c1921. The church was demolished in the 1960s.

151. The Dell, showing All Saints Church, Barnes Cray in the background, c1924.

152. The flour mill, a landmark since the 1950s, situated at Crayford Creek. The mill used to produce the special Vitbe flour for which it was once famous.

153. Barges at Crayford Creek. This idyllic photograph shows the flat-bottomed pitch-piners that transported merchandise down Crayford Creek in the early 20th century.

Crayford Marshes

Crayford Marshes

Nearing its journey's end, the embankments of the Cray were widened and raised in the 1970s, as part of the Thames Flood defences to combat the widespread flooding of the marshes in the 1920s and 1950s. As far back as the 14th Century, the Thames regularly inundated the marshes and river walls were likely to have been constructed at this time to help solve the problem.

Where the Darent joins the Cray, there is a barren landfill site on the west which was the ideal area for the storage of explosives. Indeed, the site was used by the Thames Ammunition works between 1889 and 1962. On the eastern side is an area known as Joyce Green Aerodrome, used in the First World War by Vickers for testing their aircraft. It was in a Vickers Vimy that Alcock and Brown made their first Atlantic flight in 1919. In 1917, a Vickers fighter plane was being tested at the aerodrome and crashed near the ammunition stores. Fortunately no damage was done; the pilot and plane were unscathed and simply took off to return to the airfield. One can only guess at the horror of the ammunition-workers.

Joyce Green Hospital, founded in 1902 as an isolation centre for patients with smallpox, stands 800 yards from the river on the Dartford side of the marshes. Further on, the Crayford marshes consist of hedgerows, drainage ditches and pastures with marsh flowers and birds. It is at this point that the Dartford Creek Barrier manages the river before it reaches the Thames. It was built by Sir Bruce White, Wolfe Barry and Partners in 1982 and consists of two massive concrete piers linked by a bridge 30 metres wide. Under the bridge are two falling gates, one above the other which, when dropped, can close the whole depth of the Creek, thus preventing a flood surge from the Thames.

The river, with its many facets, is held in much affection by those who know it, live by it and use it. It is a river which has seen many changes and has been changed by the industrialisation of the Cray Valley. However, the environmental consequences of this have been checked and, over the last 15 years, much has been done by Bexley and Bromley borough councils to revive the river's wild life and generate public areas where all can enjoy its attractiveness.

Along the River Cray

154. The Old Moat House of Howbury at Slade Green.
This district was mainly farmland bordering the marshes around the Cray until industrial development of the 19th and 20th centuries.

155. Annual Picnic given by the owners of Howbury Grange Farm for all their employees and families, 1905.

156. The Tithe Barn at Howbury, 2002. The wall of the Moat House can be seen on the right of the photograph. The barn dates from Jacobean times and, with its timbered roof and English bond brickwork, is a good example of the craftsmanship of those times.

157. The tidal Cray as it joins the River Darent, 2002. A Dickensian landscape despite the pylons!

Along the River Cray

158. River Darent 'helped' by the Cray opens onto the Thames. 2002.

159. Another view from the River Darent looking across Dartford Marshes towards the Queen Elizabeth II Bridge, 2002.

A pictorial history of the Cray Valley

160. River Walk, Dartford Barrier, 2002.

161. Dartford Flood Barrier, 2002. A rather ignominious end to a fascinating river trail.

Acknowledgements
During our research over several years, many people have shared information and given us assistance. We would particularly like to thank Dr John Mercer, Russell Gray, Dr Alan Tyler and other historians who have trodden this river path before us. Special thanks are due to all the team at Bexley Local Studies and Archive Centre, Simon McKeon, Frances Sweeny, Oliver Wooller, Linda McCann and Sue Barclay. We would also like to thank Gary Fairman and the Graphics Team of Bexley Council for the design of this book.

Photographic Credits:

We wish to thank the following for permission to reproduce photographs in this book.

Frontispiece: 'Cray' print. Victoria and Albert Museum

Aerofilms.com:	142
Alvis Vickers:	149
Bexley Local Studies and Archive Centre:	37-41, 43, 46, 48-50, 53, 57, 64-69, 73, 74, 76, 79-86, 88-94, 97, 99-101, 103-117, 121, 127, 129, 131-141, 143, 146, 148, 150, 152-160
Sue Barclay:	147
Bromley Libraries:	2-11, 16-22, 24-29, 31-35,
Raymond Billinghurst:	56
John Blundell, St Mary Cray Action Group:	23
Centre for Kentish Studies:	119
Crayford Camera Club:	126, 130
Walter Elms:	102
English Heritage.NMR:	12, 13, 60, 61, 71, 98
David Gillham:	151
Alan Godfrey:	44, 45, 54
Katherine Harding:	1, 14, 15, 36, 47, 72, 95, 96, 122-125, 144, 145, 161
Walter Hills:	120
Drene McDonald:	51
Philip Nash:	78
Beverley Nunns:	77
Norman Roberson, Senior:	87
Keith Turnbull Photography:	118
Kentish Times Newspapers:	75
Orpington Photographic Society:	30
Topham Picture Source:	42, 58, 59, 62, 63
Malcolm Youngs:	52, 70

Every effort has been made to trace the ownership of Photographs 55 and 128 but this has not been possible and for this we apologise.